1982

Exploring
Mime

Exploring Mime

Mime

Mark Stolzenberg

Photographs by Jim Moore

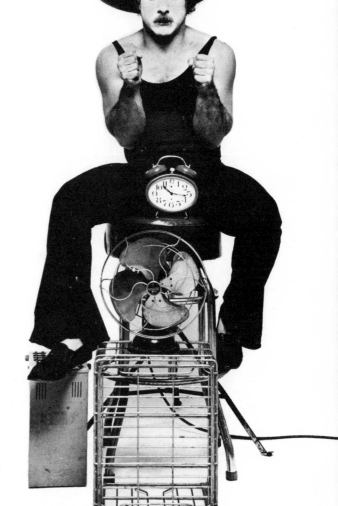

S Sterling Publishing Co., Inc. · New York

Oak Tree Press Co., Ltd.
London & Sydney

Dedicated to Edward Morganheim, my grandfather, whose sense of humor and understanding of Life helped me grow on the path to becoming an artist.

Models

Vivian Belmont
William Poag Hall
David Knox
Jay Stolzenberg
Mark Stolzenberg

The photograph on page 119 shows Mark Stolzenberg and Vivian Belmont in their New York production of "Silent Fantasies," a Mime-Clown play.

Third Printing, 1980

Copyright © 1979 by Sterling Publishing Co., Inc.
Two Park Avenue, New York, N.Y. 10016
Distributed in Australia by Oak Tree Press Co., Ltd.,
P.O. Box J34, Brickfield Hill, Sydney 2000, N.S.W.
Distributed in the United Kingdom by Ward Lock Ltd.
116 Baker Street, London W.1
Manufactured in the United States of America
All rights reserved
Library of Congress Catalog Card No.: 79-650600
Sterling ISBN 0-8069-7028-6 Trade Oak Tree 7061-2654-8
7029-4 Library

Contents

Acknowledgments

Special thanks to Vivian Belmont for her professional consultations and suggestions. Ms. Belmont's insights and technical proficiency as a mime and model facilitated the task of setting up photographs and writing this book.

I would like to thank Jim Moore for his contribution to this book as a photographer. Jim has a very special ability to capture moments and to photograph performers.

Special thanks to Beth Kehoe, my personal manager. Her conscientious, spirited and efficient efforts enabled me to find the time to write this book.

I would also like to acknowledge John Towsen, Amy Greenberg, Virginia Heath, Laurie Kaplin, Donna Cortese and Ross Elmi. And Sheila Barry, my editor, for her encouragement, patience, sincerity and sensitivity to my work.

I would also like to pay tribute to Etienne Decroux who is responsible for systematizing and categorizing Mime exercises so that Mime can be taught more easily. He laid the foundations for Mime as we know it today.

Before You Begin

Mime is the art of talking without words in a stylized way. It is a form of theatre. In Mime your body is your instrument, just as it is when you dance or take part in sports. Mime is also like dance and sports in another way. It's hard work if you want to be good at it, but it's also fun to do.

You don't have to be built in any special way to practice and perform Mime. Some mimes are tall, some short, some heavy, some thin. You do have to practice, use your imagination, and enjoy being yourself.

Why Do Mime?

There are many ways you can participate in Mime. You can do variety shows or put on full-scale performances at schools or in hospitals. You can entertain at parties or in the park. You can express your ideas and feelings, perhaps dramatize your favorite poetry in Mime. If you like to dance, you can incorporate elements of Mime into your style.

Whatever your body is like, Mime exercises will improve your coordination and help you keep in shape. When you practice the techniques in this book, you'll learn to control each part of your body, using muscles you don't normally use. This will help you in athletics and sharpen your reflexes.

Mime also helps you understand people's body language so that you can communicate more easily in ordinary life—we all talk with our bodies every day.

1
warm-ups

Warm-Ups

Before you practice Mime, you need to warm up your body. Some Mime exercises are very vigorous and strenuous. Others are gentle and soft. Sometimes you'll have to tense your muscles; at other times you'll need to relax them. Sometimes you'll have to concentrate intensely so that you can control your body. Sometimes you'll need to let loose and allow your body to do whatever it feels like doing. A good warm-up routine helps you do all this, and it keeps you from getting sore or pulling a muscle. Do the following warm-ups before each Mime session:

1. Tuck in your knees and roll easily from right to left. Do it 5 times to each side.

2. Sit on your ankles, keeping your back straight and stretch up. Do this 3 times.

3. Sit, as shown, with your left leg bent and your right leg straight. Stretch up and reach over your right leg. Your chest should sink towards your right knee. Repeat this 3 times slowly. Then do the same thing with your left leg straight and your right leg bent.

4. Do a shoulder stand, as shown. Stay in this position for one minute.

5. **The Cobra**—Lie flat on your stomach with your hands in push up position and your neck touching the floor. Slowly, leading with your head and neck, raise your back as shown. Try to feel each vertebrae in your back move up—one at a time. Keep your pelvis on the floor and use your arms for support and balance. *This is not a push up.*

Slowly come down to the floor, starting with your spine and stomach, and then lowering your chest. Finally, return your neck and head to the floor. Repeat 3 times.

6. From a shoulder stand, let your legs drop toward the floor, near your head. Keep your legs straight and only go back as far as you comfortably can. Don't strain. Then slowly unwind until you're lying flat on your back. Do this twice.

7. Lie on your back and relax. Bring your attention and thoughts to any sensations or stiffness in your body. Do this quietly for 2 minutes.

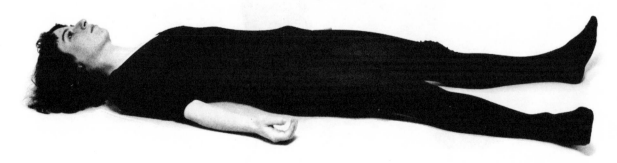

8. Roll onto your hands and knees. Contract and release your stomach and chest, as shown. When you contract (above), round your back like the back of a cat. Do this by pulling your chest and stomach muscles up and in. When you release (below), push your stomach towards the floor. Your back will then be curved in the opposite direction.

9. Get onto your feet and hang from your waist. Keep your arms and neck loose. Slowly, on an 8-count, rise, starting from your lower back, until you're standing straight. Straighten your head and neck last.

10. Do some vigorous activity—like running in place or jumping rope—until you're almost sweating.

When you do the warm-up stretches, don't strain or try to do the exercises perfectly. Do them as best you can in an easy, comfortable way.

Now you should be feeling good and ready for action!

2
the statue

The Statue

You probably played a game called "Statues" when you were young. But in Mime, being a statue is more than a fun game. When you become a statue, taking a "frozen attitude," you discipline your body, holding it perfectly still. You learn about the shape and lines of your body, and start to explore rhythm in Mime.

Run around the room, shaking out your arms and legs. Try to be really loose as you run. Make a lot of noise, too, any sounds you feel like making.

Then suddenly FREEZE. All commotion stops. Don't move a muscle. You are frozen like a rock. Try not to let anyone see that you're breathing.

Now run again and again FREEZE. Freeze in any position you land in. You should be perfectly still on the outside, like a statue. But you mustn't be a dead statue. On the inside you're bubbling with life. Imagine that you're about to explode into action, like a tiger waiting to pounce on its prey. On the inside you are vibrant with energy. On the outside you are perfectly still.

With practice, you'll be able to stay still for long periods of time. But it's important to keep the vibrations and energy going inside. This makes you interesting—exciting—to watch. Whenever you do Mime, keep that energy going inside, like a twinkle. Nobody wants to watch a dead statue!

Holding a "frozen attitude" is like holding a note in music. But the note doesn't fade. In Mime, you fill your Statue with energy and life, and the result is a performance— not just a game.

17

Some Fun Things to Try

1. The next time you go dancing, suddenly freeze in the middle of a dance. Hold that frozen attitude for a while. Check out other people's reaction to you. You'll find that you stand out in the crowd, because your stillness is so different from the activity going on around you. It proves that being still can attract more attention than moving. Stillness is a rhythm, and rhythm is an important element in Mime.

2. With a group, take turns freezing in the middle of an activity (an imagined activity—without props). For example, freeze in the middle of swinging a baseball bat. Try to freeze in a position which reveals your activity: getting dressed, lifting a weight, driving a car, running. The group can then try to guess what the "statue" was in the midst of doing.

3. Create statues which show a specific emotion or feeling (like anger, fear, pain). See if your friends can discover what feeling you're trying to express. If people have trouble guessing your emotion, figure out why and improve your statue so that your meaning is clear.

Though the mime is "frozen," there's an inner life going on that you can sense even in this photograph.

The Sculptor and the Stone

One mime is the Sculptor. The other mime is a huge slab of stone. The Sculptor uses an imaginary mallet and chisel to create and shape the Stone. The Sculptor works on one part of the Stone at a time: first the legs and feet, then the back, belly and chest, the shoulders, the arms, the hands, the neck, and last—the head and face.

The Stone must be careful to move only one part of its body at a time—the part the Sculptor is chiselling into place. The Sculptor must practice working with an imaginary mallet and chisel.

Give the Stone a name when it is finished.

Comin' Alive—An Improvisation

Look through a book of photographs of famous statues. Study one you like. Imagine you are that statue in a museum and you come to life. Before you begin, decide what your statue would want most— or look for—if it came to life: a pair of pants, for instance? A war to fight? A lost lover?

3
instant replays

Instant Replays

You've surely seen "instant replays" on TV of football, baseball, gymnastics and other sports. The plays are shown in slow motion so that you can see all the little details of the action. It's beautiful to watch and the players look very graceful.

In Mime, you don't need any special TV equipment to create instant replays. Mimes make their own by controlling their bodies and using the special rhythms of slow motion and staccato. Before you try your own instant replays, take a look at the following explanations of slow motion and staccato, and experiment with them.

Slow Motion

In slow motion there are no stops in the action. There are no sudden or sharp movements. Slow motion is mono-rhythmical; this means there is one constant slow rhythm. The rhythm never changes or varies. It stays the same, like a constant hummmmmmmmm.

When you work with slow motion, use your whole body. Try the following:

Slow Motion Experiments

1. Move any way you like in slow motion. Don't worry about doing anything special. Just have fun moving and concentrate on making your slow motion perfect.

2. Run in slow motion. Again, use your entire body. Make sure not to stop moving or make any sudden or sharp movements. Pay careful attention to the way you move from one leg to the other. You need to shift your weight gradually in order to keep the effect of slow motion.

3. In slow motion: shovel snow, throw a ball, comb your hair, hammer nails. Is your slow motion perfect?

Staccato Rhythm

Staccato movements are short, sharp, snappy, sudden, and quickly done. Each staccato move is separated from the others by a brief freeze in the action. Sometimes this freeze is very short. When you do staccato movements, it's as if a flashing strobe light is shining on you. This makes you look like a mechanical man. Or your movements may seem like separate frames on movie film.

Staccato Experiments

1. Move your arm from Position 1 to Position 2. Do it in one quick staccato movement. Then move your arm back to Position 1 in staccato.

2. Move your arm from Position 1 to Position 2 in two shorter staccato movements.

1

2

3. Run and freeze as you did when you were a statue. Move any way you like, but do it in staccato rhythm. It's a good idea, though, to move just one part of your body at a time.

4. Select one of the activities you did in slow motion and try it in staccato rhythm.

Instant Replays—Solo

Pick a sport or game you like. Mime the game without any props. Now select the part of the game you like best.

1. Perform the action in perfect slow motion.

2. Perform the same action in staccato.

3. Perform the action combining slow motion and staccato rhythms. Switch from slow to staccato, but make sure your slow motion stays perfectly slow and that your staccato is sharp, light and quick. Be careful not to mush slow motion and staccato together.

Instant Replays—Groups

Here are a few sports to try as Instant Replays. Be sure to exaggerate all your movements, using your entire body.

1. Mime a slow-motion stickball game.

2. Have a slow-motion boxing match (of course, you don't really hit each other).

3. Mime a tennis match in staccato.

4. Race a friend in slow motion. Don't be concerned with winning the race; just make it look good.

In these Instant Replays, you can create situations which are unusual, comical, or graceful. For instance, when you hit the stickball, it might go fantastically high or far. The players would wait and wait for the ball to come down. Finally it might land on the pitcher's head.

In the boxing match, exaggerate your facial expressions and reactions. Really ham it up. Make each boxer a definite character type. One might be a gigantic hulk, the other a little hustler.

On the other hand, you might want to show the grace and beauty of a boxing match or a race. You can make them dance-like—or show the determination of the athletes to win.

When you do the Instant Replays in groups, you need to cooperate closely with the other mimes, since all props are imaginary. If you're playing tennis, for instance, you have to create an imaginary ball and racquets. You and your opponents have to agree on where the ball is at all times: it can't be on both sides of the court at the same moment. Rehearse carefully with your partners so that the action is clear and an audience can follow the game.

An Instant Replay of a Steal in 4 snapshots. Try doing this with both slow motion and staccato rhythms. For example: 1. Watch the pitch come in slow motion.

2. Catch it, and discover that somebody is trying to steal home—in staccato.

3. The base runner approaches the plate in slow motion.

4. Safe!

25

4
the robot

The Robot

The "robot" is one of the most well-known uses of Mime in popular entertainment. Mimes on TV have used it; mimes in the street usually perform a "robot"; clowns in the circus do it; and even in discotheques, dancers add humor and freshness to their dancing by using some "robot" moves.

In this chapter you'll learn how to do a simple version of a robot, and in the next chapter, the more complicated "Mechanical Person." In order to perform even the most simple robot, you need to understand and practice *Neutrality,* which is a vital part of Mime technique.

Neutrality

When you perform in Neutral, you perform without projecting any character or emotion. It's similar to using "deadpan" in comedy. Your body and face should not reveal who you are or what you are feeling or thinking. Only your actions—what you do—reveal your identity and location.

Because you're not showing any character or emotion, your actions become more important. Actions in Neutral seem to be "grand" and "universal" to the audience. Your actions in Neutral appear to be the actions of Everyman or Everywoman. For this reason, the stories of myths and rituals, when they're performed on stage, are done in Neutral.

The lack of expression and character can also give the appearance of a Robot or Mechanical Person. One of the reasons why mimes wear whiteface makeup is to *neutralize* or erase their own facial expressions and personalities. This makes it easier to perform in Neutral.

The Neutral Zero Position

The Neutral Zero Position is a starting point for all your work in Mime. It is a Frozen Statue, in which you should not show any character, expression, feeling, thought, or even any action. Use the Neutral Zero Position as a home base. You will start many exercises and skits from this position. Stand as shown.

1. Keep your heels together.

2. Your feet should be open about 3 or 4 inches (8-10 cm).

3. Keep your legs perfectly straight. Don't bend at the knees.

4. Tuck in your belly and buttocks.

5. Your chest should be thrust out. Keep your shoulders back and down.

6. Attach your hands loosely to your thighs. Keep your fingers together and bend your arms slightly.

7. Keep your chin in. You should feel as though someone is pulling you erect from the top of your head.

8. Try to create a straight line from the top of the back of your head down to your ankles.

9. Relax your face and keep your mouth slightly open. If you close your mouth, you may look angry.

10. Look straight ahead at the horizon.

11. Suck in your stomach and lift your chest slightly to elongate your torso.

It's difficult to achieve the proper muscular tension for a correct Neutral Zero. If you're too tense, you'll look like a wooden soldier. If you're not tense enough, you'll look like a lazy blob. Remember, Neutral Zero is a Frozen Statue, so keep that sparkle of energy in your eyes and inner song in your heart. Every cell in your body should be vibrating with life.

*Neutral Zero
with too
much tension*

*Neutral Zero
with not
enough tension.*

Voluntary Ugliness

This is an exercise which will help you control the parts of your body which must be in position for a correct Neutral Zero. Practice it regularly.

1   2   3   4

1. Stand in a perfect Neutral Zero Position.

2. Collapse your knees as in Position 1 on page 30. Make sure the rest of your body is still in Neutral Zero.

3. Slowly let your buttocks and pelvis stick out (Position 2).

4. Collapse your chest so it no longer is up and out (Position 3). Make sure your head and neck are still straight.

5. Finally, let your head and neck drop back so that you're looking the ceiling. Let your arms dangle loosely like heavy chains n 4).

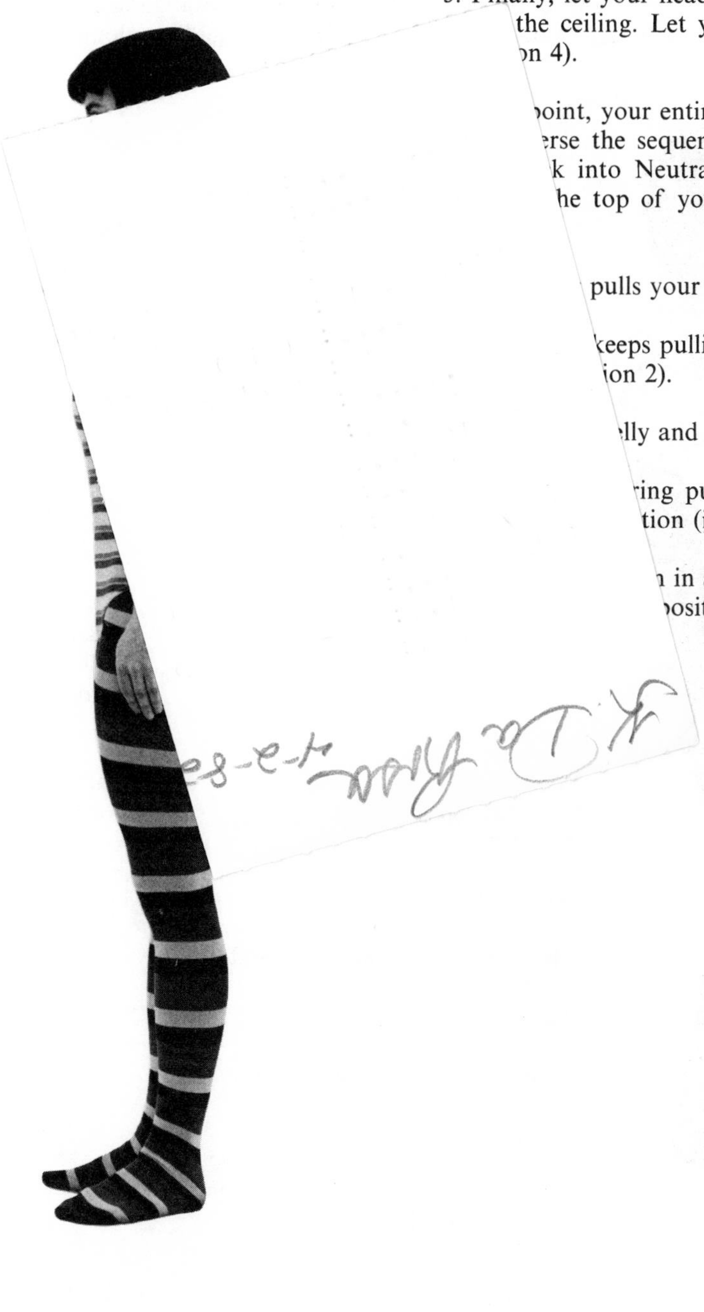

oint, your entire body is completely out of Neutral Zero. rse the sequence, so that one by one your body parts k into Neutral Zero. Imagine that someone is pulling a he top of your head which forces your body back into

pulls your head and neck back into place (Position 3).

keeps pulling. It forces your chest back to its original ion 2).

lly and buttocks straighten out (Position 1).

ring pulls your knees straight, and you're back in tion (illustration to the left).

in a mirror or have a friend make sure you're osition.

The Simple Robot

Now that you can maintain the Neutral Zero Position and understand what Neutrality is, try a simple robot:

1. Stand in a perfect Neutral Zero Position.

2. Little shuffling steps will propel your robot. Keep your feet close to each other and slide them very briskly across the floor. Make sure to keep your entire body in Perfect Neutral Zero alignment. Move only your feet. You should look as if you're gliding along the floor.

3. Now try making sharp turns to the right and left. The sharper you make your turns, the more you'll look like a machine.

4. Pivot on your heels and do a sharp about-face. Struggle to keep your robot's body in Neutral as you turn. Remember, don't allow yourself any facial expression.

Robot Improvisations

The Run-Away Robot

Start from the collapsed position of the Voluntary Ugliness exercise on page 30. Imagine that you are a robot which needs to be wound up.

Someone activates your motor and you start to move into Neutral Zero: first your head and neck.

Wait a few seconds.

Next, your chest moves up and out.

Pause.

Your belly and buttocks tuck in.

Pause.

Last, your legs straighten and you begin to chug around the room.

At first, all is well and you avoid any obstacles by making sharp turns. Then your radar breaks down and you begin to bump into things: walls, chairs, people, whatever. Rotate briskly in a circle. Finally you break down altogether. Collapse into the position you started in. Your owner comes along and carries you off for repairs.

What is the robot doing to show that she is a broken machine rather than a dead—or sleeping—body? Note that her head and neck are stiff, her eyes open. Her arms show muscular tension rather than hanging limply. Her back is straight.

Bumper Cars

Do the Run-Away Robot improvisation with 3 or more people. Then, when your radar breaks down, you can bump into each other. Bounce or spring away after you bump into another robot.

Before you attempt the bumper car effect, carefully practice bumping into each other. Decide upon the points of impact beforehand.

5
the mechanical person

The Mechanical Person

In order to create a more complicated robot, or Mechanical Person, you'll need to practice some basic Isolation exercises. You'll be able to apply these *isolations* to many of the improvisations and skits in this book.

Isolations

Practicing isolations for Mime is like practicing scales in music. Isolations are a system of exercises which help you develop control of the various parts of your body.

When you *isolate* a part of your body, you move it alone without involving any other part. When you do an *isolation,* you move that body part in a specific direction and to a definite rhythm—just as a musician practices scales in a definite rhythm. Your body is your instrument in Mime.

You can isolate many parts of your body:

> your head
> eyes
> neck
> shoulders
> chest
> waist
> pelvis
>   and buttocks
> upper arms
> lower arms
> upper legs
> lower legs
> hands
> feet
> fingers
> toes

Here you'll be doing three kinds of isolations: Rotations, Inclinations and Translations.

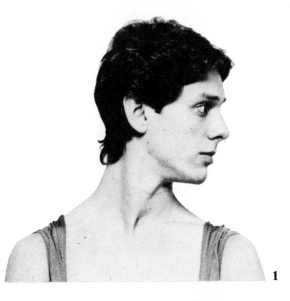

Rotations

Turn a part of your body around the central axis of your spine and neck. Imagine a bead on a string. The string (if you hold it straight), is like your spine, and the bead is like your body part. You can spin or turn the bead around the string (illus. 1).

1

Inclinations

Tilt a part of your body without rotating it. If you stand in Neutral Zero and look down at your feet, you'll be inclining your head and neck downward. If you try to touch your right shoulder with your right ear—without moving your shoulder, only your head and neck—you'll be inclining your head and neck to the right (illus. 2).

2

Translations

Slide a part of your body to the side without rotating or inclining it. The body part moves parallel to the ground (illus. 3).

3

37

Rhythm

Because you can't speak in Mime, your rhythm will speak for you. Rhythm talks, and everything you do in Mime is done to a particular rhythm. Therefore, it makes sense to practice isolations in different rhythms. In all of the improvisations and routines you do, try to use variations in rhythm to communicate what you're thinking and feeling.

Here are a few of the rhythms you'll be working with as you practice.

Tuc

A single, sharp, staccato movement, like the sound of a finger snap. Tucs should be sharp and light—brisk.

Slow Motion

See page 21. Slow motion is like a long continuous hummmmmmm, similar to the effect created by the soft pedal of a piano.

Tuc-Echo

A combination of staccato and slow motion. First you perform a Tuc movement. Then you continue the same movement in slow motion. The effect is like a loud noise followed by an echo. When you strike a cymbal, you get a Tuc-Echo effect.

Magic Starts and Stops

Begin and end your movement without any tension. Try not to show the beginning of the movement. Start it gently and magically. When the movement comes to its end, let it die out slowly so that the audience hardly notices that it has stopped.

Cause and Effect

Sometimes moving your chest causes your arms to move. At other times, moving your arms causes your chest to move. These movements are "Causes" (the Cause triggers off other movements); the movements that result are "Effects." For instance, in the Tuc-Echo rhythm, the Tuc is the Cause and the Echo is the Effect. If you lift your shoulders up, your arms and hands move up also. Your shoulders are the Cause, your arms and hands the Effect.

Isolation Scales

Practice the following isolations regularly. Begin from a Neutral Zero Position and move only one part of your body at a time. Everything else should remain in Neutral. Check yourself in the mirror.

These isolations will help you create an interesting Mechanical Person and develop your control of your body.

Head and Neck Rotations
Right and Left

1. Rotate your head to the right—to the eighth (illus. 1). (The eighth is a position between center and profile. The profile position is often called the "quarter.")

Rest a second. Rotate your head back to center. Do the same to your left. Repeat this 4 times to each side in slow motion and 4 times to a Tuc rhythm.

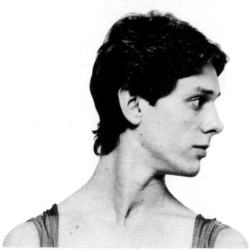

2. Next, rotate your head with a Tuc to the right. Stop at the eighth, and with another Tuc, continue the rotation to your profile (illus. 2).

When you rotate your head to your profile, the movement involves your neck. Then wait a moment. Rotate your head back to the eighth. *Pause*. Now rotate your head back to center. In each one of these rotations, use a Tuc rhythm. Do the same thing to your left. Repeat this 4 times to each side.

39

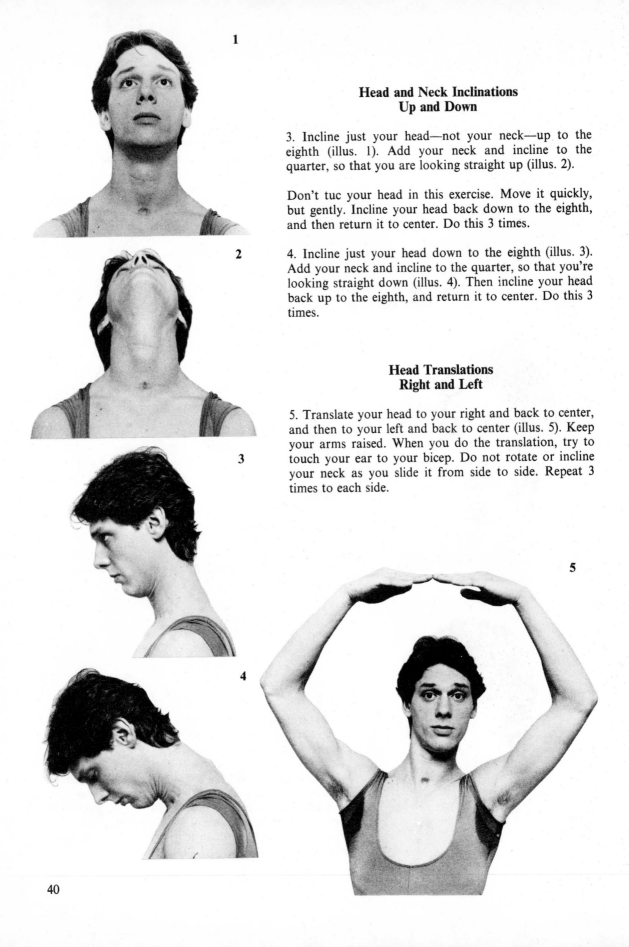

Head and Neck Inclinations
Up and Down

3. Incline just your head—not your neck—up to the eighth (illus. 1). Add your neck and incline to the quarter, so that you are looking straight up (illus. 2).

Don't tuc your head in this exercise. Move it quickly, but gently. Incline your head back down to the eighth, and then return it to center. Do this 3 times.

4. Incline just your head down to the eighth (illus. 3). Add your neck and incline to the quarter, so that you're looking straight down (illus. 4). Then incline your head back up to the eighth, and return it to center. Do this 3 times.

Head Translations
Right and Left

5. Translate your head to your right and back to center, and then to your left and back to center (illus. 5). Keep your arms raised. When you do the translation, try to touch your ear to your bicep. Do not rotate or incline your neck as you slide it from side to side. Repeat 3 times to each side.

Head in Cross

Use a Tuc rhythm and wait a moment between each Tuc. Move your head to the eighth, as follows: Right, center, left, center, up, center, down, center. Do the sequence 4 times.

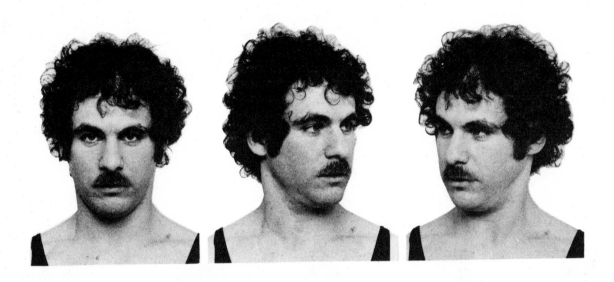

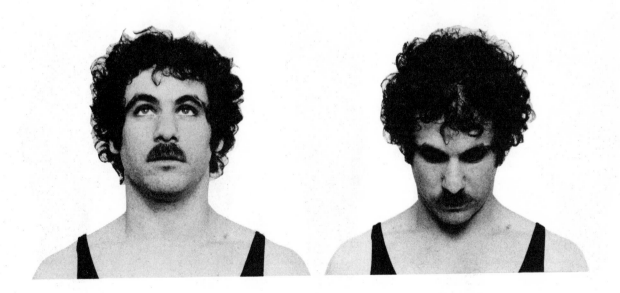

Shoulders

Begin in Neutral Zero. Move both shoulders up and down to a Tuc rhythm—4 times (illus. 1-2).

Now do it with your right shoulder alone. Then with your left shoulder alone. Be careful not to move your head, neck, or chest as you work with your shoulders (illus. 3).

Rotate your right shoulder forward in a circle (up, front, down, back). Do the same with your left shoulder. Repeat 4 times with each shoulder (illus. 4-5).

1   2   3   4   5

Eyes

There are muscles in your eyelids which, normally, you don't control consciously. In Mime you need to use them to help you express your feelings, intentions, and to reflect what you see.

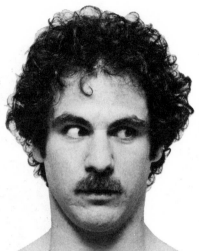

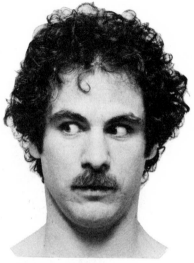

1. Stand in Neutral. Widen your eyes. Just move your eyelids, not your eyebrows or forehead. Now relax your eyes. Do this 6 times.

2. Widen your eyes. Shoot them to your extreme right in a Tuc rhythm. Then shoot them back to center.

3. Now shoot your eyes to the extreme left and back to center.

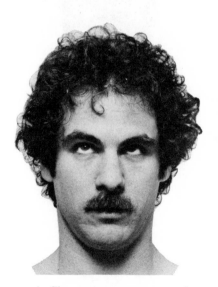

4. Shoot your eyes up and back to center.

5. Shoot them down (look at a spot about 6 feet in front of you) and back to center.

Some Tips

Select a clear center point to focus on. Always come back to the same center point.

Make sure you don't move your head or shoulders while you work with your eyes.

Do the exercise 6 times. Speed up the rhythm the last 2 times.

As you master this exercise, you'll be able to hold your eyelids open for longer periods of time.

Chest Inclinations—Right and Left

Try not to incline your waist in this exercise; only your chest should move.

Do it 4 times to the right and then to the left.

Stand in Neutral. Lift your chest and separate it from your waist.

Slowly incline your chest to your right. Your head and neck should remain in line with your chest.

Now incline back to center. Check yourself to make sure you've returned to a good Neutral Zero Position.

Chest Inclinations—Forward and Back

Start in Neutral. Again separate your chest from your waist.

Incline your chest forward and then back to center.

Incline your chest back and then back to center.

Repeat 4 times, keeping your head and neck in line with your chest. When you incline back to center, check for a good Neutral Position.

Translations of the Chest

In all of these translations, try not to involve your waist, and keep your head and neck in line with your chest. Do not incline or rotate as you translate!

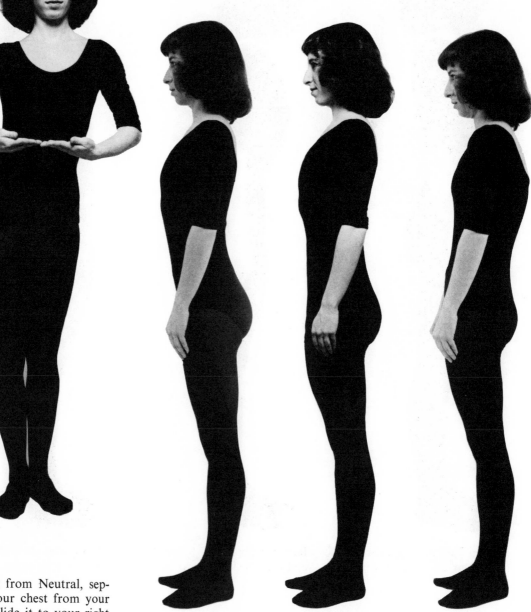

Starting from Neutral, separate your chest from your waist. Slide it to your right and back to center. Then slide it to your left and back to center. Do this 4 times to each side.

Translate your chest forward and back to center 4 times.

Translate your chest back and to center 4 times.

Rotations of the Chest

In all these chest isolations, your chest is the Cause and your head and neck move along with it. Your head and neck should remain in line with the center of your chest.

Starting from Neutral, separate your chest from your waist.

Rotate your chest to the right and then slowly bring it back to center 4 times. Do the same to the left.

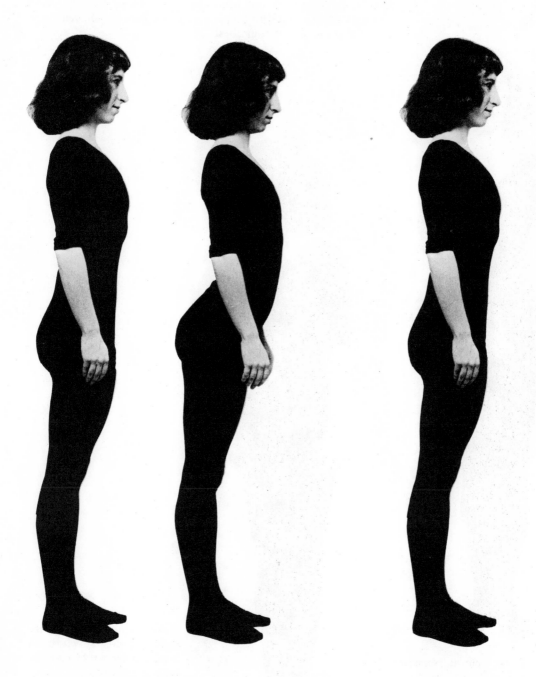

1. Start in Neutral (First Position). Now allow your pelvis and buttocks to stick out, as shown. Imagine that two hot pins are approaching your pelvis and buttocks.

2. Your buttocks retreat back to the Neutral tucked-under position to avoid the hot pins. Repeat 4 times in First Position, Second Position, and Fourth Position (see page 49).

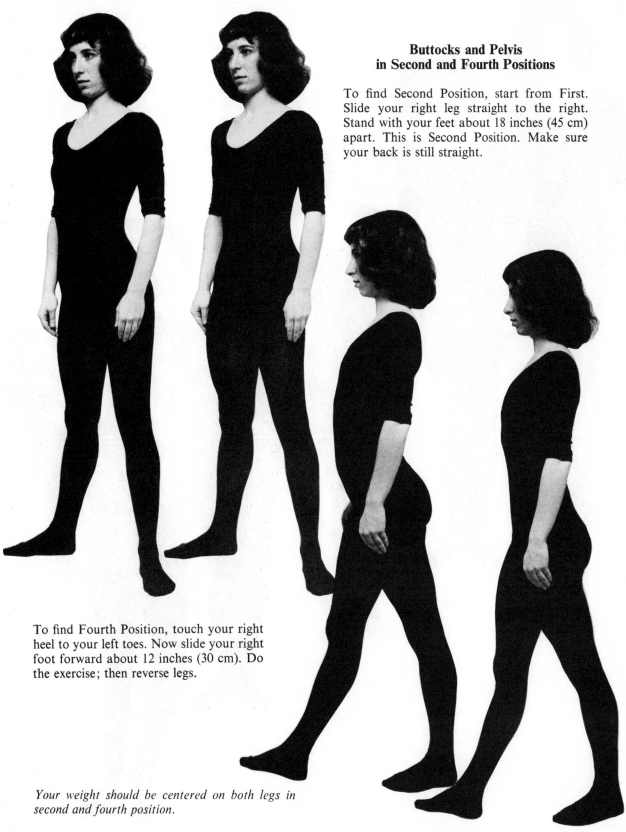

Buttocks and Pelvis
in Second and Fourth Positions

To find Second Position, start from First. Slide your right leg straight to the right. Stand with your feet about 18 inches (45 cm) apart. This is Second Position. Make sure your back is still straight.

To find Fourth Position, touch your right heel to your left toes. Now slide your right foot forward about 12 inches (30 cm). Do the exercise; then reverse legs.

Your weight should be centered on both legs in second and fourth position.

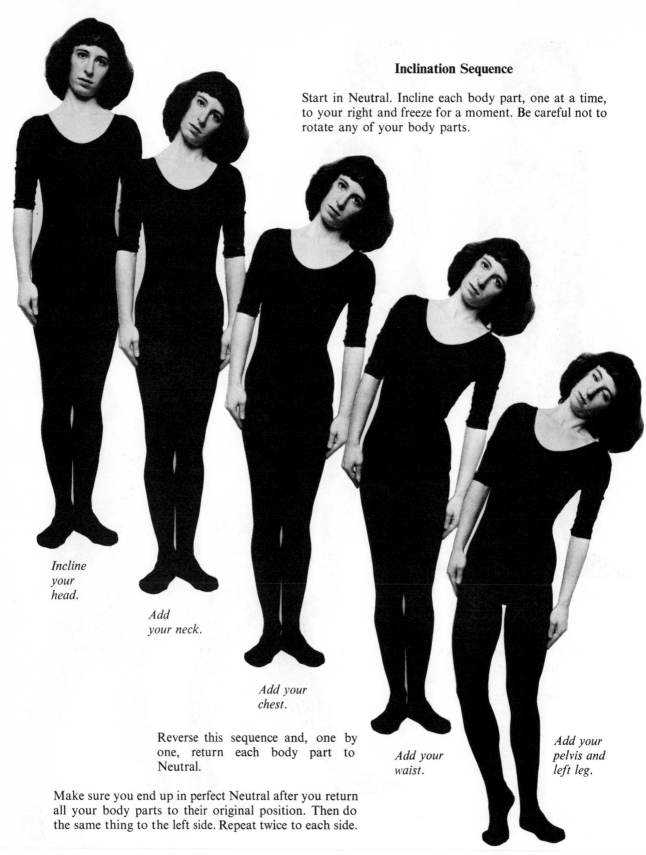

Inclination Sequence

Start in Neutral. Incline each body part, one at a time, to your right and freeze for a moment. Be careful not to rotate any of your body parts.

Incline your head.

Add your neck.

Add your chest.

Reverse this sequence and, one by one, return each body part to Neutral.

Add your waist.

Add your pelvis and left leg.

Make sure you end up in perfect Neutral after you return all your body parts to their original position. Then do the same thing to the left side. Repeat twice to each side.

Rotation Sequence

Again move each body part separately, this time in rotation. First rotate to your right.

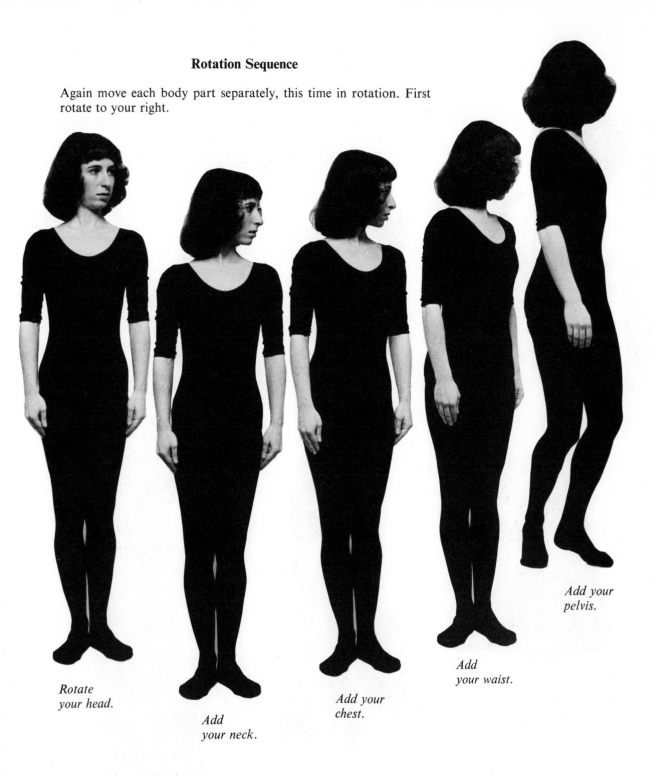

*Rotate
your head.*

*Add
your neck.*

*Add your
chest.*

*Add
your waist.*

*Add your
pelvis.*

One by one, return each body part to its original position. You should be back in Neutral now. Do the same rotations to the left and then return to Neutral. Repeat twice to each side. Make sure you don't incline as you rotate.

Creating the Mechanical Person

When you create a mechanical person, try to break down your movements into simple isolations. You can use isolations of your head, neck and chest as you walk and reach for things. A mechanical person *cannot* curve his or her spine in a smooth rhythm.

Stand as shown.

Rotate your head from right to left and back to the right. Continue this movement with your head as if you were a machine:

Right-left-right-left-right-left . . .

Rotate your head in slow motion, but add a little Tuc when you reach the extreme left and extreme right. The Tuc causes your head to change directions. This is a Tuc-Echo rhythm (see page 38).

While your head is rotating from side to side in a continuous Tuc-Echo rhythm, move your arms forward and back to the same Tuc-Echo rhythm. Note that when you rotate your head to the right, your left arm is forward and your right arm is back. As your head rotates to the left, your arms should reverse their positions. This may be easier if you imagine that your head and arms are connected to the same gear. The change in direction of your head causes your arms to switch positions.

For a mechanical walk, take little tiny shuffling steps, as you did in "The Robot," or you can try sliding your feet along the ground as if you're on a track. If you slide your feet, make sure to coordinate your steps with your arms: as your right arm comes forward, your left leg comes forward. When your left leg slides forward, your right arm should be moving forward.

As a Mechanical Person, try these activities:

1. Sit in an armchair.

2. Get a drink of water from a faucet.

3. Deal cards for a poker game.

4. Hand out leaflets in a shopping center (an imaginary shopping center, of course).

The Shooting Gallery—An Improvisation

Three or four mechanical people are targets in a shooting gallery. The targets shuffle about. When a rifleman makes a hit, the target does a series of isolations, indicating it has been hit. When the target returns to normal, it spins around and then continues to shuffle along. Suddenly, the targets get angry and freeze. They mischievously look at each other, deciding to rebel. They attack the riflemen.

Each target should have its own series of isolations to perform when it is hit. It can use the same sort of isolations for the final attack.

More Improvisations and Skits

1. You are a door-to-door salesman who sells robot maids. Give free demonstrations with your sample maid.

2. You are the manager of a factory where all the employees are mechanical people.

3. You are the first mechanical person allowed to compete against real people at the Olympics.

4. You are a mechanical detective programmed to track down criminals.

These are just a beginning. Experiment with them. Explore all the possibilities, even if they seem far out. Then find other situations you can work into dramatic and comic scenes. More about creating skits in Chapter 14.

6
the traffic cop

The Traffic Cop

Have you ever watched traffic cops who are very involved in their work? Some of them are hilarious to watch and they enjoy putting on a show for passersby.

You can create funny routines using the action and situation of directing traffic. The character of the traffic cop can be dramatic and entertaining.

Because traffic cops rely heavily on their hands to direct traffic, you need to practice arm and hand isolations before you can explore a skit. You'll be using the same isolations for many other purposes, too.

The Windmill

1. Stand in Neutral.

2. In staccato, move your right arm from diagonal-down to diagonal-up.

3. Move your left arm from the diagonal to the horizontal.

4. Combine the two and move both arms together.

While you do the windmill, keep your arms locked (straight). Repeat 5 times.

57

Fold-Up Arms

Start in Neutral.

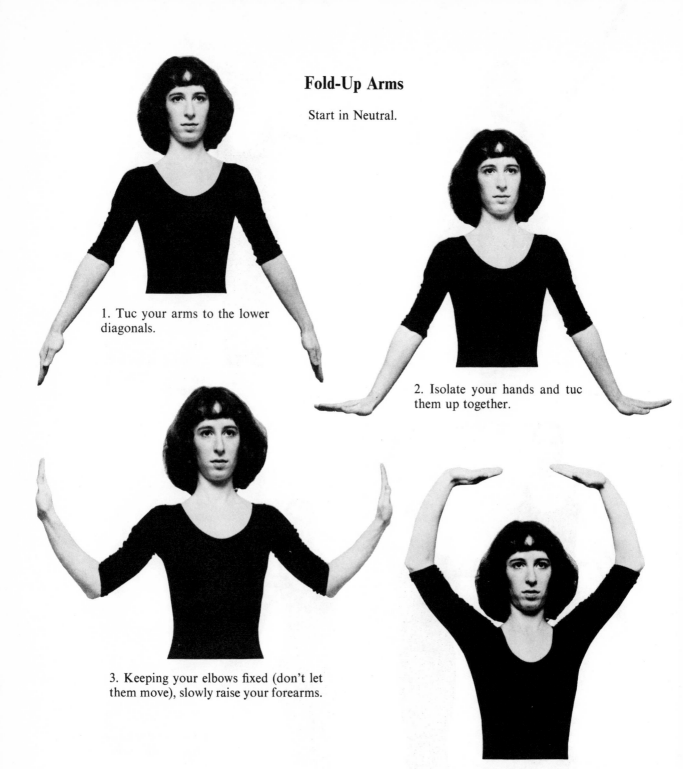

1. Tuc your arms to the lower diagonals.

2. Isolate your hands and tuc them up together.

3. Keeping your elbows fixed (don't let them move), slowly raise your forearms.

4. Keeping your shoulders fixed, explode your entire arm up to the next position.

When you have completed the sequence, reverse it and return your arms to the starting position. Repeat 3 times.

The L

This exercise is called the L, because you carve
an imaginary L in space with each arm.

1. Begin with your arms straight
and perpendicular to each
other.

2. Simultaneously, slide your
left arm *across* and your right
arm *down* to the next position.

3. As your arms approach each other, they tuc and
change direction, as if an electric charge made them
repel each other. Your left arm slides up and your
right arm slides out to the side.

4. Continue the exercise—in
reverse—returning to your original position (illus. 1).

Repeat 4 times.

Caress the Stick

Imagine that a broomstick is resting across your shoulders. Your arms are supporting it.

Caress the underside of the stick with the backs of your hands as you bring your arms in.

With 2 consecutive Tucs, first slip your right hand over and then your left, so that your palms are facing up.

Slide your arms back out, caressing the stick with your palms.

60

Slide your arms back in. Caress the stick with your palms.

Flip your hands around again. Now your palms will be down.

Caressing the stick with the back of your hands, return to the starting position.

Allow your arms to sink slowly to your sides.

Do the sequence 4 times.

61

Hands

1. Stand in Neutral with your hands hanging limp. Shake your hands up and down from the wrist briskly.

2. Move your hands into tight fists.

3. Stretch each finger out directly in front of you in a fan-type motion.

4. Start with your pinkie and move each finger back. End by clenching your thumbs into a tight fist again.

Traffic Improvisations

Imagine you're directing traffic during rush hour at a busy intersection. Wear a police cap and white gloves, if you can get them, to help you feel the part.

Before you begin the improvisation, work out specific stylized signals using your arms and hands for the following:

STOP	WAIT A MINUTE
GO	YOU! PULL OVER.
SLOW DOWN	HEY, WHERE DO YOU
SPEED UP	THINK YOU'RE GOING?

Try directing traffic as a musical conductor might direct an orchestra. Use many different rhythms. Really see the specific cars and people you direct.

For example:

> A huge truck comes by. The driver is a little old man with a big cigar. He has trouble turning the corner because his eyesight is bad. You help him make the turn.

> A wealthy lady in the back of a big limousine stops in the middle of the intersection to ask directions.

> Three cab drivers stop to pick up the same passenger. There is a violent argument which you settle. Meanwhile, the passenger has taken the bus.

React to the sight and sounds of the intersection—horns honking, pedestrians crossing, young people, old people. What kind of day is it? What is the weather like? Do the exhaust fumes annoy you?

Should Have Stayed in Bed—An Improvisation

> You are handling the rush hour crowd efficiently, and you're proud of it. Suddenly an old lady trips and falls in the street. You help her up and through the intersection. When you return to your post, you find a big mess of a traffic jam. Six drivers are out of their cars, fighting and arguing. Horns are honking. You break up the fight, give out a few tickets, and get the intersection back to normal. You see a good-looking woman or man, proudly tip your hat. While you are flirting, a dog uses your leg for a hydrant. As you bend to tend to your pants, a bicyclist accidentally bumps you in the rear, which sends you flat on your face. You lie in the middle of the street, and let out a huge sigh, as if to say, "I should've stayed in bed."

Ideas to Work Out on Your Own

> 1. Direct traffic in a blizzard.

> 2. Someone runs a red light and refuses to stop when you whistle.

> 3. A milk truck stalls in the intersection and you help push it out of the way.

7
the wall

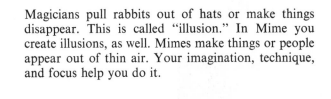

The Wall

Magicians pull rabbits out of hats or make things disappear. This is called "illusion." In Mime you create illusions, as well. Mimes make things or people appear out of thin air. Your imagination, technique, and focus help you do it.

Many illusions in Mime work best if you perform them *in face:* facing the audience directly or with the front of your body parallel to the front of the stage. Other illusions work best if you perform them in *profile:* facing the wings of the stage, with your profile to the audience. Still others will be most effective if you perform them on a *diagonal* (between face and profile).

Test out illusions in front of your friends or a trial audience to figure out in which angle or position they are the clearest and most believable to the audience.

The wall is probably the most popular illusion in Mime. It's pretty easy to do, and you'll really create the illusion of a wall, if you do it properly. Before attempting the wall illusion, though, you need to work on the isolation of creating a fixed point in space.

Hands Fixed

Place your right hand in front of you as if it were on an imaginary table. Imagine that it is firmly glued to this *fixed point in space.* When a point or part of your body is *fixed,* that means it doesn't move. It is stuck in space.

Move your body in various directions, but don't allow your hand to move.

Struggle to free yourself in every direction, but you cannot.

Pull in every direction, including up and down.

Note that, as you pull away from your hand, your right arm straightens. As you move toward your hand, your right arm bends.

Do the same thing with your left hand.

Find different positions or places at which you can fix your hand. Struggle to pull away each time. Use your entire body.

Fix both hands in space. Struggle to pull away. Be careful not to move either hand.

Creating the Wall

The wall is most clear when you perform it in face, though you can do it in profile or on a diagonal as well. First decide exactly where you want your wall to be. Define the space. Run your hands along the wall. Make sure it is flat and straight. Know where it begins and ends. What is it made of? What color is it?

Open your hand and reach out to the wall, gradually spreading your fingers. When you are about to place your hand on the wall, your fingers should be spread apart and almost straight.

Then, with a Tuc, place your hand on the wall. There should be a lot of muscular energy in your hand, as it tucs against the wall. Your fingers should stay spread. Your hand should be parallel to your chest and straight.

Gradually relax your fingers as you withdraw your hand from the wall. Relax your hand completely before you approach the wall again.

Select a nearby spot on the wall. Place your hand there with a Tuc. Now pick another spot. Keep your hand relaxed when it is not on the wall. Do this a few more times.

Try it with your left hand. Select different heights at which to place your hand.

Make sure your hands are parallel to your body when they are on the wall.

Once you establish the wall, keep it consistently in the same plane. Be careful not to tilt your hands; this will make the wall slant. Try to create a straight wall without curves or bumps.

Keep looking at the wall. Create it in your mind and imagination. You don't have to look at the exact spots where you place your hands, but when you have both hands on the wall, look between them.

Next, place both hands on the wall directly in front of you. Without moving your body, release your right hand and place it to the extreme right on the wall.

Now release your left hand and place it next to your right.

Keep your hands *fixed* in this new position. Step to the right so that your hands are directly in front of you again.

Repeat this several times. Then do the same thing going to your left.

69

Explore the same procedure going up and down, instead of to your right and left.

Place both hands on the wall above your head. Now move your hands down a few inches lower on the wall—one at a time. Bend your legs and lower your body until your hands are again at the height of your head. Keep your hands fixed as you bend.

Now place your hands higher. Fix your hands there and straighten up to your original position.

Exploring the Wall

Experiment with your wall, varying your rhythm. At some point, move away and then towards the wall, while you keep your hands fixed on it.

Try to push the wall (it won't budge). Lean on it. Punch it.

The Shrinking Room—An Improvisation

Create the four walls of a room. Suddenly, the walls and ceiling begin to close in on you. You struggle to push the walls away. Even the ceiling is getting dangerously low. You are about to be crushed when you discover a tiny door. Open it and crawl out to safety.

Ideas for Group Improvisations

1. Paint a wall with another mime. Find slapstick conflicts with your paintbrushes and buckets.

2. Build a wall with a group of mimes. Each mime should be in charge of a different operation. Use wood, bricks, cement, plaster boards. Hang a big poster or billboard on the wall when you're finished.

3. Create a huge box. Move it around the room without letting it change shape.

8
the witch's brew

The Witch's Brew

Here you'll cook a huge cauldron of soup. In order to do it, you'll need to handle and manipulate many small imaginary objects. Before you start, warm up your hands (see page 62).

This recipe requires the following imaginary equipment and ingredients:

Huge cauldron of water
Fire to cook on
Large Stirrer
Cutting Board for vegetables
Knife for cutting vegetables
Spoon for tasting the soup
Carrots
Potatoes
Celery
Onions
Salt and Pepper shakers
Herbs
Serving Ladle
Bowls for the soup
Anything else your imagination
    wants to conjure up

Practice creating and handling each item. Try to create the object so vividly that an audience will recognize it.

To create and cook a carrot, for example: Hold the carrot in your left hand, keeping your fingers together. Keep the shape of the carrot in your hand. Your carrot should be a little bigger than a real carrot, so that it's easier to see and handle. Take a bite out of the end of the carrot. Pick up a big knife. Follow the length of the blade with your eyes. Touch the tip to check its sharpness and length (with staccato rhythm). Pull your fingers away swiftly and lightly. Now you are ready to cut the carrot. Hold it on your cutting board and chop with short, sharp, staccato movements. When you toss it into the soup, follow it with your eyes. See it plop into the pot.

Cooking Tips

When you first grasp an object—or when you release it—use a slight Tuc of your hand.

Use different rhythms for different activities. Cutting, stirring and tasting, for example, each call for a different rhythm.

Create surfaces (counter tops, bowls, plates) carefully. Are they flat or curved?

Focus is important when you work with imaginary objects. Make sure there are no other activities going on which will distract the audience.

Show how you feel about each ingredient you cook. Does it smell bad or good? Your performance will be more interesting if you feel strongly.

Use your entire body wherever possible.

Exploring Soup—An Improvisation

Cook a huge magical cauldron of soup. Cook it carefully; everything must be done according to your witch's handbook. The soup is done. You taste it and it is perfect. Look around for a victim to try your brew. An innocent mime comes by on his daily walk. Call him over and offer him a hand-out. He cannot resist, since the soup looks and smells so good. He takes a few sips and suddenly goes into convulsions, turns into a frog, and hops about. Laugh at your accomplishment. Spill some soup on the frog's head and he slowly returns to normal. When the innocent mime gets his senses back, he wonders what happened. How did the soup get on his head? He walks off, bewildered.

Exploring Small Objects

When you handle small objects, always try to be clear. Exaggerate the size of the object. Vary your rhythm, and use your entire body as much as possible. Try:

1. Getting dressed

2. Dealing cards

3. Lighting and smoking a cigar

4. Throwing a tennis ball into the air and catching it

5. Making up your face

6. Playing a flute

9
the weightlifter

The Weightlifter

So far you've explored the creation of imaginary objects and circumstances—illusions. But how can you show how heavy or light an object is? It's important to establish the weight of imaginary objects; it helps to create a believable illusion.

Here you'll learn two different techniques for creating the illusion of weight. With them, you'll be able to act out a well-known and funny skit called "The Weightlifter."

Mimes are forever struggling against gravity, as opposed to dancers who seem to defy gravity. Boxes, chairs, glasses—even balloons—have weight. The mime has to handle heavy objects, clumsy objects, immovable objects—walls or perhaps even elephants. The mime's struggle against nature can be tragic or comic or both at the same time.

The most important thing to remember when you try to create the illusion of weight in Mime is to show the weight in your body. The technique is called "Counterweight." With it your body reflects the weight you're lifting, carrying, pulling or pushing. For example, these pictures show the mime holding two different boxes. You can see him showing the weight of the boxes with his body.

There are two basic ways to show weight in Mime. The first is called *counterweight to the rescue*. In this counterweight, you use your body to help you move or resist weight.

In the picture at the left the mime is pushing against the wall. Notice that she is leaning towards the wall and using her body to help her push.

Try it yourself. Create a wall which cannot be moved. Try to move it. As you push, lean towards the wall. Use your chest to help you.

Counterweight to the Rescue

Counterweight in Retreat

The second method is called *counterweight in retreat*. Here your body retreats from your working arms and hands. This gives you the power to push, lift, or resist the weight.

In the picture at the right, the mime's body is moving away from the wall as she pushes against it. Note that her chest is concave.

Try it yourself. Use the *counterweight in retreat* to push the wall. Make sure your chest is concave and that your hands and arms are the Cause (pushing). Your chest and body are the Effect.

Moving a Piano—An Improvisation

Move a piano with 3-5 people. Make sure you agree about the exact size and shape of the piano, where it begins and ends. Work together as a group. Some people push the piano; others pull it. Try to be aware of what the other piano-movers are doing. Use both counterweights—retreat and rescue. Use your entire body. Slide the piano across the room.

Weight Improvisations

Explore the following activities and then work up a short skit using one of them. Pay special attention to creating a counterweight. Use your chest and legs to support the work your arms and hands are doing:

1. Throw a shot-put.

2. Play a game of bowling. (Exaggerate your reactions)

3. Dig a ditch.

4. Carry a heavy suitcase to the airport.

Pumping Iron—An Improvisation

Stand in second position, as shown. Flex your muscles. Let the audience know how strong you are. There is a huge barbell (imaginary) at your feet.

Look at it.

Grasp the bar with one hand at a time.

Try to lift it twice, but you can't.

The barbell drops back to the floor with a thump. Notice how the mime's chest is retreating in this picture.

Look at the picture sequence on the next pages as a guide to the rest of the skit. Make sure you create the tremendous struggle of handling the weight.

9

10

11

12

13

You need to think as a weightlifter might think when you do this skit. In other words, create a character. This is an example of what you might be thinking as you lift the barbell.

1. This is the third try. It's not going to fall this time, I hope.
2. Got it!
3. Uh-oh . . .
4. Push up with the right hand, it falls down on the left.
5. Push up with the left, it falls down on the right.
6. WHEW!
7. My feet are slipping. . . . Stay cool in the face of danger.
8. I can't allow this to continue. . . .
9. Ha! I did it!
10. Very carefully. . . .
11. . . . put it back down.
12. How about that!

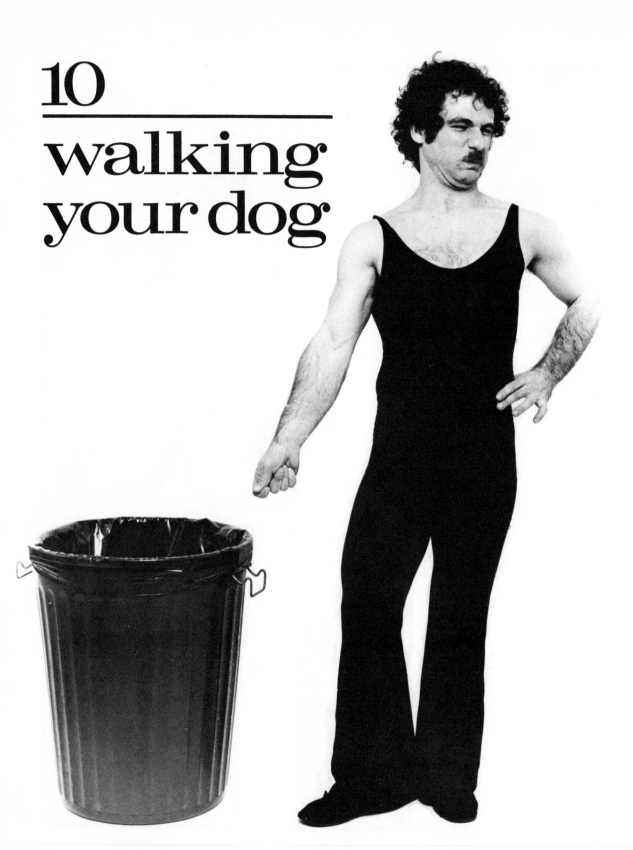

10
walking
your dog

Walking Your Dog

Mime dogs are a pleasure to own. They're intelligent, friendly, cheap to take care of, and they will not mess up your house or chew on your furniture. All you have to do is convince an audience that your mime dog exists.

In order to walk your dog, you need to work on *pulling and being pulled by an imaginary force*.

Raise your right arm to the horizontal.

Imagine someone or something is pulling your right hand to your right. Keep your arm straight.

Resist this force by pulling to your left.

85

Repeat this a few times, as if you were having a tug-of-war with the imaginary force.

Finally the force overpowers you and pulls you away.

Do it to the left with your left arm. Vary the rhythm. Sometimes you struggle against the force in slow motion. At other times you must use staccato tugs or jerks to win the tug-of-war.

Your First (Mime) Dog—Improvisations

Close your eyes and imagine a dog. What color is it? What breed? What is its name? In your imagination, watch the dog playing in the park. Study its rhythms.

Open your eyes and imagine you're walking your dog on a leash. If your dog is big, take large steps as you walk. If your dog is a frisky little puppy, take small staccato steps.

Reflect the rhythm of your dog in your own walk. Walk with your arm bent. When your dog pulls on the leash, use the principle of being pulled. Your arm should straighten when the dog pulls you.

Perform the same tug-of-war in many directions.

Dog Trouble—An Improvisation

It's a beautiful spring day and you're walking your dog in the park. Stop and throw a stick for him to fetch. Suddenly you realize you have a date with a friend and you're late. You put your dog back on the leash and head for home. Your dog meets another dog and they stop to check each other out. Anxiously you tug on your dog; he will not budge. The other dog and its owner walk away and your dog pulls after them. Struggle with your dog. You're very late. Your dog gets away from you and catches up to the other dog. Their leashes get tangled. You can't untangle them, so you cut your leash with your pocket knife and carry your squirming dog home.

Ideas for Skits

1. Someone asks you to hold on to his absolutely tremendous dog while he goes into the supermarket. The dog drags you through the street. You can't control it. It knocks people over, stops traffic, refuses to obey you.

2. Someone asks you to watch his tiny dog. The dog is so small you can hardly see it. It runs away and hides in different places: under cars, under a lady's dress, behind trees. Explore the possibilities!

3. Explore an improvisation called "A Day in the Life of a Dog-Catcher."

11
mime
walks and runs

Mime Walks & Runs

As a mime you can create an entire universe without moving from a small area on stage. There are stylized walks and runs which allow you to cover great distances while remaining on one spot. Here you'll learn two types of Mime walks and a way to run in place.

To walk and run in Mime, you need to use your legs in a special way. Here are some leg isolations which will help you use your legs properly. Use a dance barre or the back of a chair for support.

Flexions

A flexion is like a knee bend. In all flexions, make sure the line from the top of your head to the bottom of your spine is straight. Your chest should be out as in Neutral. Be careful not to incline backwards as you sink down. Your leg muscles will be working hard, but don't let the effort show in your upper body and face. You should appear at ease and natural from the waist up.

First Position

Your feet are in Neutral. Do 4 demiflexions (as in the illustration at the right). Your heels remain on the ground, flat-footed. If your heels come up, it means you've gone down too far.

Now do 4 deep flexions. In deep flexions, your heels come up, but keep them together in First Position.

Second Position

Do 4 demi-flexions and 4 deep flexions in this position.

Fourth Position

Do 4 demi-flexions and 4 deep flexions in Fourth Position (see page 49 for a description of Fourth Position).

The Brush

Make sure you don't incline to the left.

Start from Neutral. Translate your weight to your right leg. As you shoot your left leg forward, carve an imaginary line on the floor with your toes.

Keep your left leg absolutely straight, like a spear. *Brush* the floor with your toes as you slide the foot forward, pointing your foot gradually. It should be completely pointed when your leg reaches the extreme forward position.

If you move your foot too far forward, your pelvis will begin to slide forward, out of place. Try not to let your pelvis move at all.

Now, leading with your heel, thrust your left leg back towards Neutral.

As your left foot meets your right foot, bounce it off your right foot—like a springboard—and shoot it out to the side, as in the illustration to the right. Again, carve an imaginary line with your toes directly to your left.

Bring your left foot in again, leading with your heel. As your left heel touches your right heel, rebound your left heel off to the back, as shown below.

Carve a straight line to the back. Point your toes behind you.

Try to keep your pelvis and buttocks tucked in.

Now put it all together. Brush your left leg as you did before—to the Front—Side—Back—Side—and return to the Front. Repeat this 6-10 times, beginning the sequence slowly and speeding up.

Turn around and hold the barre with your left hand. Do the same thing with your right leg. Remember to keep all your weight on your left leg, so that your right leg is free to move. Don't incline backwards.

In all the brushes, look straight ahead. Don't let the effort show in your face and upper body. Try to look at ease.

The Walks

The two walks you'll find here are "The Profile Walk" and the "Inclination Walk," a walk in face. Both are walks in place. That means you don't literally walk or move forward, but you give the illusion of walking.

The Profile Walk—leg movements

1   2   3   4   5

The Profile Walk

1. Begin in Neutral. Slide your right leg forward as in The Brush.

2. Lead with your heel and slide your right leg back to Neutral. As you slide your right leg back, flex your left leg and raise your left heel (#2).

3. Straighten your left leg, sliding it out in front of you. Your weight is now on your right leg (#3).

4. Slide your left heel back, flexing your right leg. Bring your right heel up (#4).

5. Straighten your right leg and start again (#5).

Do this sequence slowly at first. Struggle to keep your moving leg straight, your head at the same height. Try not to bounce up and down.

The Profile Walk—arm movements

10   9   8   7   6

Arm movements: Your arms should move in opposition to your legs. This means that your right arm will be forward when your left leg is forward. This opposition movement is natural. It is the way your arms and legs generally move when you walk.

Your wrists should lead the movement of your arms. Never lead with your fingers. Look at the picture sequence on page 97. Pay careful attention to the stylized arm movements. Work slowly on coordinating your arms and legs. With a little practice, you'll be able to do the Profile Walk in a continuous, smooth rhythm. Remember always that your intention is to walk *somewhere*. Look straight ahead at your goal.

The Inclination Walk

1. Stand in Second Position.

2. Incline your body to your right. Make sure that your entire body inclines in one piece. The only thing that should break the straight line of your body is your right leg, which bends. Bring your right heel off the ground. For now, keep your arms at your sides.

3. Incline back to Second Position.

4. Incline to your left.

5. Come back to center again.

Incline again to your right. This time, squeeze your right heel down to the ground as if you were squashing a rubber ball. The squeezing of your heel is a Cause. It triggers you to incline your entire body to your left—the Effect. Now squeeze your left heel and incline back to the right. Repeat this many times. The result is a sauntering kind of walk.

To improve the illusion of walking:

Lift your foot slightly off the ground just before you incline to the side. It's like taking a small step *in place*.

You can walk in place slowly or quickly. In either case, keep your chest out and look straight at your goal.

The Inclination Walk—body and leg movements

Try to show the spirit, feeling and intention of walking. Imagine that you're actually going to something and covering distance. Imagine things you might pass as you walk—buildings, people, trees, animals.

Look at these pictures to see how your arms should move in the Inclination Walk.

Running in Profile

Stand as shown on page 101. You are in the attitude of running. Your intention is to move forward to your goal. Your arms are in opposition, whenever you walk. Your chest should be caved in.

Hop twice in place on each leg. You are now doing a Mime run. You continue hopping twice on each leg to give the illusion of running.

If you want to speed up, hop 4 times on each leg quickly.

If you want to run even faster, hop 8 times on each leg.

Speed up your rhythm as you increase the number of hops. When you switch legs, switch the position of your arms.

Keep your chest concave and look straight ahead. Remember that
this is a run—not an exercise in hopping! Try to show the feeling
and attitude of running by constantly focusing on your goal.

Off and Running

After you've practiced the walks and the run, try them while
imagining the following:

1. You are in your house.

2. You are in a large gymnasium.

3. You are in a beautiful garden (don't step on the flowers).

4. You are walking in the rain.

5. You are running to catch a friend.

6. You are running away from a bee.

In order to perform a skit that calls for much walking or running, you need to work on the movements until you can do them very easily and naturally. During the skit, you'll want to concentrate on achieving your aim as a character: for example, the aim of the weightlifter might be to impress a pretty girl at a carnival. If you haven't mastered the walk or run, you will be too involved in technique to be able to concentrate on who you are and what you want (See page 112 for more about character).

The Picnic—An Improvisation

You are going for a walk in the woods with a picnic lunch (the inclination walk). You find a suitable spot and sit down to eat your sandwich. Suddenly, several bees attack you. You run away (run in profile). Finally, in a clearing, you escape the bees. You enthusiastically sit down to eat. After your first bite, you hear thunder. You pack your things and run to the nearest road (run in profile). As you walk home (profile walk), it begins to rain. Run home as fast as you can.

You can perform this entire skit within a few square feet.

12
the astronaut

The Astronaut

How do mimes show that they are hot, cold or wet? Mimes must be able to sense imaginary conditions, react to them, and make that reaction physical in a stylized way (See Chapter 13 for more about style).

Here you'll learn how to sense and communicate hot and cold. You can use the principles you learn to work with other imaginary conditions and stimuli—and you can also use them to be The Astronaut.

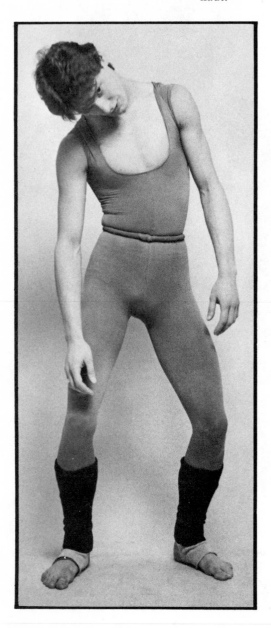

Sensing and Showing Heat

Walk around the room in an easy, relaxed way. The room is getting hot. You are becoming more and more uncomfortable as you walk. Decide what the heat is coming from: is it the sun? a radiator?

You begin to sweat. Feel the sweat drops trickling down your back and on your forehead. Loosen your shirt. You move slower and slower. Your body becomes loose and slouched. Wipe away the sweat. You are dizzy and exhausted from the heat. Finally you faint.

Sensing: The trick in sensing the heat is to be specific. Imagine small details, like sweat drops or bright light in your eyes. The more specific you are, the better. For instance, it's better to imagine *a big sweat drop in your eye* than to imagine merely that you're sweating.

Showing or Projecting: It isn't enough to sense the heat. You must show it with your body. Do this by finding parts of your body which are affected by the heat and determining exactly how they are affected. For example, your mouth becomes dry, so your tongue begins to hang out. You are becoming tired, so your legs seem very heavy and you have trouble lifting them. Find actions to deal with the condition, like wiping away sweat drops or fanning yourself. Your rhythm can show that it is hot, too; everything slows down.

The mime is using his whole body to project the sense of heat, not just indicating it with a gesture.

Sensing and Showing Cold

Walk around the room as you did before. First work on sensing. Where is the cold coming from? How cold is it? What parts of your body feel cold first? How does your body react? *Be specific.* As you continue the exercise, concentrate on showing or projecting the cold with your body. Do you move faster or slower? Is your rhythm slow or staccato? Find actions—rubbing hands together, putting on your coat. Does your body do things in the cold which you can't control?

The Astronaut—An Improvisation

Sit in a real chair. You are an astronaut. Your job is to explore an unknown planet, but before you blast off, you'd better familiarize yourself with your ship:

Where are your controls?

How do they work and what do they do?

How do you communicate with Earth?

Are you travelling with a co-pilot?

How long will you be gone?

What does the inside of your ship look like?

When you know your ship, take off. After three days, you land on Planet X in another solar system. You explore the planet and discover that half the planet is unbearably hot and the other half is unbearably cold. What kinds of things might you encounter on the hot side? On the cold side? You take samples of the terrain and return to a splash-down on Earth.

More Heat and Cold

1. Build a snowman.

2. Go ice-skating or skiing.

3. Improvise a day at the beach.

4. Take a hot bath.

13
style - lookin' good

106

Style—Lookin' Good

Style is what makes Mime and Pantomime different from Silent Acting. In Mime and Pantomime, you use your entire body—not just your face and arms and hands. Your spine and chest help to project and exaggerate the character, emotion or action that you are trying to create and add intensity and depth to the visual image you present. If any part of your body is not working with you, it detracts from that image.

Look at this photograph. The mime is indicating with his hands, arms and face that he is afraid.

In this photograph the mime is creating the fear with his entire body. He is depending less on facial gesture to show his fear. This is the result you want—in Mime.

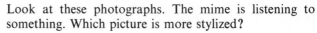

Look at these photographs. The mime is listening to something. Which picture is more stylized?

The second photograph (right) is a better way to listen in Mime, because the mime's whole body is involved. It is more stylized. The style helps the audience see and understand what you're doing from far away. It also makes your movements more interesting, unusual, attractive, exciting, and enjoyable to watch.

Activities—Stylized

First do the following activities in a realistic way—the way you actually might do them in life. You can discover what this is by trying the activity with real objects. Then take the objects away and do the same movements as if they were there. Finally, stylize the activity.

1. Sewing

2. Shooting with a bow and arrow

3. Cooking an egg

Remember to use your whole body and add the tension or muscular energy of Mime to your actions. Exaggerate the size of your movements, the size of the objects. Work on your rhythm so that your action is clear. For example, use staccato movements when the needle and thread get stuck and when you first stick the needle into the material. Show the release of the arrow with a tuc forward of your chest and head. Reflect it with your glance in slow motion. As the arrow comes down, slowly come down from your toes. As the arrow hits the target, land on your flat feet with a tuc; also tuc your head to indicate the impact of the arrow.

Emotions—Stylized

Tie a scarf around your face—or wear a blank mask—and create the following statues, using your entire body:

1. Anger

2. Fear

3. Pain

4. Joy

See if your friends can tell what your emotions are.

In real life or in other forms of acting, it is possible to show emotions in many, many different ways. But in Mime, it is important to stylize the emotion so that it will project all the way to the back of a large auditorium. The guidelines here will help you express your emotions within the style of Mime.

Anger: *Your chest is out. Your weight is going forward on your front leg. Fists are clenched, muscles tensed.*

Fear: *Your chest is concave. Your weight shifts backwards away from the thing which is frightening you. Your head is also retreating.*

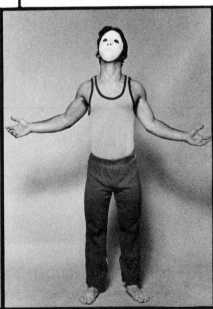

Pain: *Your entire body curls around the area which hurts, as if to protect it.*

Sorrow: *Your chest and stomach collapse. Your legs bend a little. Your head inclines down. You can use your hands around your face to indicate grief.*

Joy: *Your body is very open and relaxed. Your chest is slightly forward, but not as far as in Anger. Your arms are open. Your head is inclined back slightly towards the sky.*

14
creating skits

Creating Skits

In Mime you have the opportunity to create your own stories and express your own ideas and feelings. All good theatre makes some kind of statement about life and the world we live in. If you have any special ideas or strong feelings about people, nature, or the universe, you can create a Mime skit around them.

You have two basic elements to work with when you create your own skit: character and plot (or story).

Character

When you portray a character, ask yourself the following questions:

1. Who am I?

2. What do I want?

3. List the details of the character: age, sex, occupation, temperament (grouchy, pleasant, warm, timid, whatever).

4. Where does the character live?

5. Is the character rich, poor, in between?

6. Is the character athletic, brainy, or both?

7. What animal is like this character?

8. What food reminds me of this character?

Then try to create the character with your body.

1. How does the character stand?

2. How does he/she walk and run?

3. Is the character fat or thin? Tall or short?

4. What is the character's rhythm like?

5. List 5 important words that describe your character. For example, lonely, young, inexperienced, shy, sweet.

Select a few activities to try as the character: play ball, drive a car, sing, dance, dress.

If you explore your characters thoroughly, using a checklist such as this, it should make it easier to play them in skits or stories.

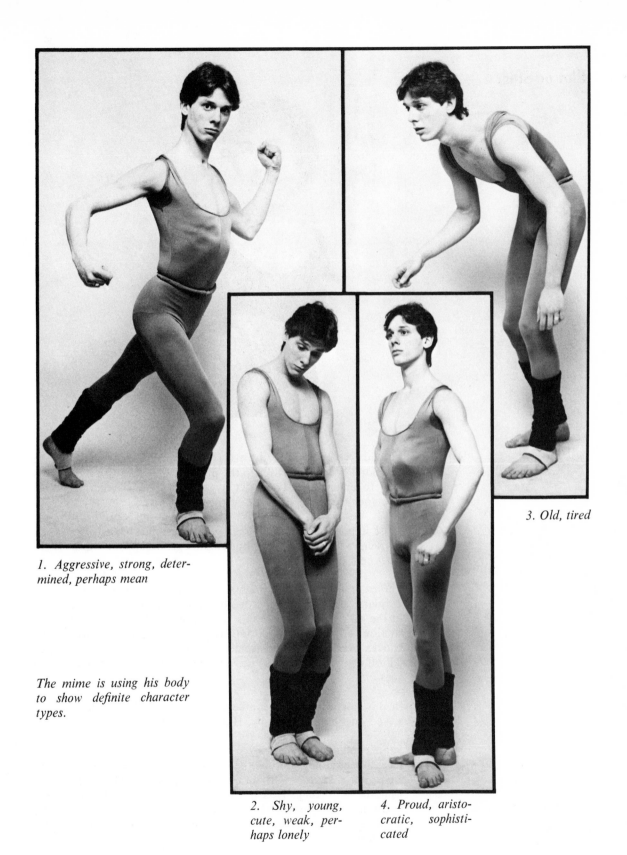

1. Aggressive, strong, determined, perhaps mean

The mime is using his body to show definite character types.

2. Shy, young, cute, weak, perhaps lonely

3. Old, tired

4. Proud, aristocratic, sophisticated

113

Plot or Story

In Mime you should try to make your stories pretty simple. Since you don't have words to help the plot along, you need a plot that is easy to understand. Don't let it get too complicated. It helps to give your story or skit a title or theme.

Most important to the plot is conflict. Conflict takes place when characters want something but cannot get what they want. There must be a problem.

For example: a young woman is pledging a sorority and must burglarize a house as part of her initiation. She is terrified, but agrees to the task because she wants to be accepted. After sneaking in a window, all kinds of things go wrong. She trips in the hallway. She knocks over a lamp. She accidentally turns on a radio. Her glasses fall off in the dark and, as she searches for them, the burglar alarm goes off.

In this story you find a conflict—or problem. The problem can be solved or it might end sadly. How would you end it?

Some conflicts can be funny. For example: a young man is getting ready for an important date. He is nervous. Everything goes wrong. He tries to take a shower, but there is no hot water. He rips his pants while he is dressing. He can't find one of his shoes. He leaves the house and then realizes he forgot to put on his socks. When he finally arrives at his date's house, he finds out she is ill and cannot go out tonight.

In both of these plots, there is a conflict because the characters want something but can't get it due to obstacles. Another kind of conflict takes place when a character has two actions to perform which can't be done at the same time. For example: a teenager takes his girl-friend to the movies with the intention of fooling around a little in the back row. The movie turns out to be really interesting, a super murder mystery. At one point the boy can't decide whether to kiss his girlfriend or watch the movie. He really would like to know "who done it," but at the same time, his very attractive girlfriend isn't resisting his attempts to kiss her. He solves his conflict by borrowing her makeup mirror and holding it behind her head so that he can see the movie in the mirror while he is kissing her.

There is another type of conflict, one in which the aims of the characters interfere with each other. For example: One mime is the lion tamer. Another mime is a lion. The tamer is very proud and macho. He wants to make a big impression on the audience. The lion has eaten a horse tranquilizer which one of the circus hands accidentally dropped near the lion cage. The lion tamer tries his best to put on a good show, but the lion only wants to sleep—no matter how much it is prodded.

    The lion tamer wants to put on a great show.
+The lion wants to sleep.
=CONFLICT.

Mime skits should have a title, a beginning, middle and an end. For example, in the movie skit:

Title—THE DATE

Beginning—should introduce the main characters and perhaps reveal their intentions. THE DATE might start with the couple waiting in line for the movies.

Middle—the development of the story. The middle shows the characters carrying out actions to achieve their aims or goals. The conflict appears.

End—The conflict is either resolved or left unresolved.

Ideas for Skits

Fairy tales are a great source of skit material. Try "Hansel and Gretel" or "The Three Little Pigs." You can perform the story in Mime and use narration on tape or live to help fill in details or background.

Legends are another good source. How about "Robin Hood"? Here you would definitely need narration. Use it to explain things which you can't show in Mime. For instance, if you want the audience to know about King Richard, who is off fighting a war, use narration to explain the situation.

15
makeup

Makeup

Before the invention of electric lights, theatres were lit by candle-light. Actors often put white flour on their faces and outlined their eyes with black charcoal so that the audience could see them better. One of the reasons why mimes wear whiteface is so that the audience can see them. The white makeup makes their facial expressions stand out.

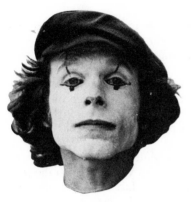

Another reason for wearing whiteface is that it identifies you as a mime. You are able to draw attention to yourself more easily. This is especially useful if you're performing outdoors, where you want to capture people's attention quickly.

However, it's not essential to wear white makeup to perform Mime. In fact, many mimes prefer not wearing whiteface. Some mimes just outline their eyes with a black grease pencil and add a little rouge to their cheeks.

Here are the items you need to apply a whiteface:

1. White pancake makeup

2. Makeup sponge

3. Black grease paint or pencil

4. Makeup brush

5. Red grease paint

6. Baby powder and powder sock, powder brush

7. Baby oil to remove the makeup

8. Tissues

9. Mirror

You can buy these items in a store that carries theatrical makeup. They are usually listed in the classified pages of your telephone directory. Sometimes magic stores carry makeup supplies, too.

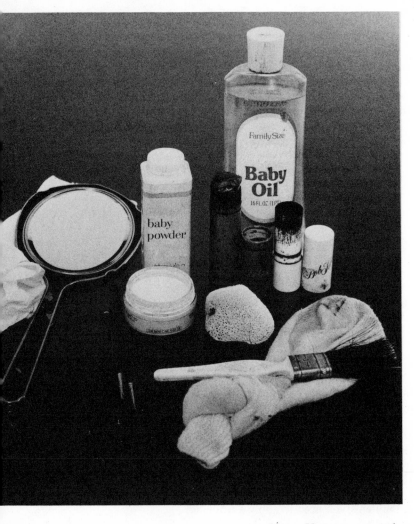

To apply the makeup:

1. Dampen the sponge in water and dab it into the white pancake makeup.

2. Apply the white generously to your face. Cover your entire face, including your eyelids and eyebrows. Don't miss any spots. Spread it around so there are no streaks. Tap it with the sponge to make the surface smooth.

3. Apply the red grease paint sparingly to your cheeks and/or lips with your finger or with a brush.

4. Use a brush to apply black grease paint to create new eyebrows above your own and to line your eyes. Or use a black makeup pencil.

5. Fill a white athletic sock with baby powder. Tap your face with the sock until your face is covered with powder. Brush away excess powder with the powder brush. The powder will set your makeup and keep it from running.

6. Use baby oil or Albolene cream to remove the makeup, after the performance.

Note: You can use red or black to create simple shapes which can be your trademark—like a tear, a triangle, or a red circle on your cheek. But be careful not to overdo it. If you put more than two or three small shapes on your face, it will be busy-looking and interfere with your facial expressions.

When you work on creating your makeup, bear in mind that your normal face is unique. Don't try to cover up or hide your face, but use the lines and muscles you naturally have. When you finish putting on your makeup, look in the mirror and make faces. Try to discover the effect your makeup has on your expressions. How does the makeup make you feel? You should be comfortable and pleased with the designs, shapes, and overall image that the makeup gives you. Experiment with variations: make one eyebrow different from the other, or change the angle and position of lines or shapes. A simple adjustment in the angle of a line (under your eyes, for example), might make you feel much better about your makeup and help you express yourself.

16
performing

Jim Moore, performing in the streets of New York.

Photo by John W. Retallack.

Performing

You might perform in many different places or situations—at parties, before a mime class, in the park or on stage. In all cases, it is important to rehearse thoroughly. Know exactly what you will be doing and work out most of your movements beforehand. Both you and your audience will get the most out of your performance if it is well-rehearsed and planned.

Using Improvisation

Let's say you're working on a skit about Robin Hood. It would be helpful to explore the different activities Robin might be involved in. By improvising with these activities (eating, hunting, riding a horse, etc.) you'll determine which activities lend themselves most readily to Mime and to your talents. Improvising will also help you develop your characterization and work out the story.

When you have improvised thoroughly, it's time to make decisions about which actions and movements you want to include in the performance. It helps to show your skit to friends at this point to find out if they see what you want them to see. If you're riding a horse, for example, and four or five spectators don't see a horse and just think you're dancing or jumping up and down, you have to make it clear that you're riding—or eliminate this action completely.

Creating skits is often trial and error, but by the time you're ready to perform, you should know exactly what all your movements will be.

Parties

If you're asked to perform at a party, bear in mind that most parties are fairly informal and you may want to improvise more than usual. You can imitate people at the party, make believe you are someone's dog, or freeze like a statue—perhaps "becoming" a door or a piece of furniture. If you do a skit, make sure your audience is seated and attentive. A Mime audience must be quiet and watchful in order to understand and appreciate skits.

Whatever you do, keep it short and simple. You can try things like the wall illusion, the Weightlifter, the Robot, or a very short comic skit. Four or five skits are plenty; your performance should last from 15 to 20 minutes.

It's useful to find out beforehand exactly what your performing area will be like, so that you can prepare for it. You may be cramped into a small space.

In the Street or Park

Select a performing area where there will be the least amount of distraction; parks are usually preferable to the street. Define your area carefully: know where you want to perform and where you want the audience to be. Try to manipulate the onlookers so that they stand where you want them. Very short skits and simple illusions work best outdoors. Don't attempt a subtle or complicated scenario; there are too many distractions for that.

Note: Find out what the attitude of the police is to street performers before you begin. In some places, street performing is welcomed; in others, it is illegal and you could get a ticket.

On Stage

Here you have the greatest control over your environment. You can use lights and music, but make sure that they serve your performance. They shouldn't detract from it or dominate it. You may want to use a simple set or costume. If you work in costume, make sure it doesn't hide the lines of your body. Often just suggestions of a costume work best—like hats, gloves, glasses, scarves—these little things add character, but don't mask your movements.

Performing Professionally

If you're serious about wanting to be a mime, see as many Mime shows as you can. Keep a log book of ideas, notes and observations about Mime and skit ideas. Find a Mime teacher whom you respect and who makes you feel at ease and take as many classes as possible. If you can't find a Mime teacher in your vicinity, take ballet lessons or jazz or modern dance classes. Acting and theatre courses are also important. If you want to perform professionally, you need to study long hours for many years.

Mime in Perspective

Mime is the art of speaking with the body using a specific and stylized technique. There are many different styles of Mime, including rituals, elements of Eastern Dance, Commedia dell' Arte, Lecoq Technique (used by Mummenschanz), Silent Acting, and French Classical Mime (20th Century). This book has focused on French Classical Mime, since it is the most popular system today and the foundation on which most contemporary western Mime is based.

The word Mime (with a capital M), has referred to the Modern French Technique which was created and developed by Etienne Decroux, Marcel Marceau's teacher. The word mime (with a small m) refers to the actor who performs Mime or Pantomime.

Mime is different from Pantomime. Mime refers to the system of exercises, technical strategies, dramatic movement sequences, dynamics and punctuations which Etienne Decroux developed in his search for an "essential theatre." Pantomime is the use of elements of Mime to convey a story. The genius of Marcel Marceau was in applying Mime technique and style to create character and plot in Pantomime.

Decroux's concept of theatre was to strip it down and use only those elements which were necessary to the theatre. His research led him to the conclusion that, of all the elements of theatre, only the actor is indispensable. He then discovered that even words were not necessary, since the actor's movements and attitudes could replace words and, at the same time, convey a more deep-rooted and underlying meaning than spoken language. So came the creation of Mime or theatre without words.

A layman watching Mime might at first glance think it were dance. A mime might be dressed in leotards and tights, performing without the stereotype whiteface makeup. Often in Mime, the story is not very literal; it might be abstract. Mimes are graceful (like dancers) and many of the conventions are similar (pointed toes, disciplined body alignment). But on closer observation, the spectator would see that Mime is different from dance in several ways:

1. The style of Mime is rooted, grounded, tied to the earth. This conveys a sense of tremendous struggle. Dance, in comparison, is much more weightless and airy. The dancer leaps and defies gravity; the Mime is tragically bound by it.

2. Mime deals with essence. The Mime strives to create with a minimum of movement. Only that which is absolutely necessary is used. Dance, in contrast, is decorative. The dancer does arabesques, pirouettes, and repeats patterns for the sake of a visual aesthetic, for the sake of beauty.

3. Mime is theatre and drama first and movement second. Dance is a movement discipline which is *sometimes* dramatic and theatrical.

4. Mime is a new and undeveloped art form in comparison with Dance, which has been cultivated for centuries.

This book has dealt with both Mime and Pantomime. Mime is silent theatre, expressionistic and transcendental in that it often deals with the hidden and underlying meanings and forces in the universe. Pantomime addresses itself to character and plot, relying heavily on the creation of imaginary objects and people to convey a story.

Mime, if studied seriously, can uplift the Mime actors and give them an increased understanding of themselves, others, and the world we live in. The treasure of Mime and Pantomime is that they also provide a vehicle to present this understanding to others in a theatrical and entertaining way.

Mime—but it does sometimes look like dance

Guide to Technical Exercises

1. Warmups

2. The Statue
The Frozen Attitude

3. Instant Replays
Slow Motion
Staccato

4. The Robot
Neutrality
Neutral Zero Position
Voluntary Ugliness

5. The Mechanical Person
    Isolations:
    Rotations, Inclinations,
      Translations: head, neck, shoulders,
      eyes, chest, buttocks and pelvis
Rhythms: tuc, tuc-echo,
      magic starts and stops, cause and effect

6. The Traffic Cop
    Arms: The Windmill, the L, Fold-up
      Arms, Caress the Stick, Hands

7. The Wall
Hands fixed
Tension and Release

8. The Witch's Brew
Manipulating small objects

9. The Weightlifter
Counterweight—Retreat and Rescue

10. Walking Your Dog
Pulling and Being Pulled
Reflecting Rhythms in Your Walk

11. Mime Walks and Runs
Flexions (pliés) demi and deep
Positions (1st, 2nd, 4th)
The Brush
Profile Walk
Inclination Walk
Run in Profile

12. The Astronaut
Sensing and Projecting Heat and Cold

13. Style—Lookin' Good
Stylizing actions
Stylizing emotions

14. Creating Skits
Character
Plot
Conflict

If you are teaching Mime yourself, begin each class with the exercises in the first three chapters. These are basic and should be repeated every time you teach or practice.

For younger students, a 45-minute Mime class is sufficient; 90 minutes is a good length for an adult class. Set aside time at the end of the class for improvisations (from 15 to 30 minutes).

Glossary

Cause and Effect   A *Cause* is a movement which initiates another movement. An *Effect* is a movement which results from the impulse of a prior movement or a *Cause*.

Conflict   An essential element of most plots, conflict results from the clash of opposing objectives. Two characters may want conflicting things, or one character may have a conflict within him or herself. Whenever an obstacle stands in the way of a character achieving an objective, there is conflict.

Contract and Release   To tighten a muscle group and then relax it.

Counterweight   An element of Mime technique which projects weight and gravity by reflecting these forces in the body.

Echo   Usually a slow movement which is a response or the result of another movement.

Face (in face)   Performing Mime facing the audience and parallel to the front of the stage.

Fixed Point in Space   An imagined point which is stuck in space and cannot move or be moved. This point may be outside or inside the mime's body.

Flexion   Similar to a knee bend, very much like a plié in dance.

Frozen Attitude   A frozen attitude is created when a mime freezes in the middle of an activity. In the frozen attitude, one of the most fundamental aspects of Mime, the mime is still like a statue. The lines, curves, and muscluar energy of the mime project a meaning.

Illusion   The stylized creation of imaginary objects in Mime. Illusion also refers to the compression or expansion of space in Mime.

Improvise (improvisation)   To act out a skit extemporaneously, to create a skit or actions spontaneously around a theme or simple idea.

Incline (inclination)   To tilt a part of the body to the side, front or back without rotating or translating it.

Intention   What a character wants to do.

Isolate (isolation)   To move a specific part of the body in a predetermined direction and with a specific rhythm without moving any other body parts.

Magic Starts and Stops.   A punctuation of a movement in which the movement starts and ends imperceptibly.

Manipulate (manipulations)   To create and use imaginary objects in Mime. For example, small objects and tools are "manipulated" with your hands.

Mime   The art of speaking with the body using a specific and stylized technique. A form of silent theatre.

mime   An actor who performs Mime.

Neutral   Without character or emotion—blank. Neutrality in Mime is like a blank screen on which the mime and the audience can project images.

Neutral Zero   A basic position in Mime similar to First Position in ballet. In Neutral Zero there is no character, emotion or action.

Objective   An acting term referring to what a character wants.

Pantomime   The art of conveying a story or plot using Mime technique and characterization.

Profile (in profile)   Performing at a right angle to the audience; on a proscenium stage, facing the wings.

Project   In Mime, using muscular energy or tension along with acting technique to clearly convey your meaning over a distance to an audience.

Reflect   To show with the body. The mime "reflects" the size, shape and meanings of objects and people with his or her body.

Rhythm   Changes in the speed and tension of movements which punctuate and clarify meanings in Mime.

Rotate (rotations)   To isolate a part of the body by turning it around its axis without inclining or translating it.

Silent Acting   A style of acting without words, as in silent movies or as in silent moments in the speaking theatre. Not to be confused with Mime, which is more stylized.

Slow Motion   Moving slowly at a perfectly constant speed.

Staccato   Sharp, light quick movements followed by a freeze.

Stylize   To add the projection, tension and body rhythms specific to the Mime technique.

Technique   A system of exercises and rules of projection. In Mime, Decroux technique is very popular. Technique provides a language to create with.

Tension   Physically, the muscular energy used to project in Mime.

Translate (translation)   To isolate a body part by sliding it to the side or forward and back without rotating or inclining it.

Tuc   A sharp staccato accent.

Whiteface   A form of theatrical makeup with a white base. It is often used by mimes and clowns.

Index

About the Author

Featured on the cover of *New York Magazine* for his highly acclaimed performance in the two-mime drama "Silent Fantasies," which he co-authored with mime Vivian Belmont (also pictured in this book), Mark Stolzenberg has been electrifying audiences in just about every theatrical medium. After studying acting at the Herbert Berghof Studios and Mime with several different teachers over a period of five years, he attended Ringling Bros. Clown College, and subsequently was chosen to clown with Ringling Bros. Barnum & Bailey Circus. He has made numerous television appearances, acted in films (he co-wrote and played a lead role in "Clowns," a 1920's style silent film), and on stage in many roles (including the one-man, one-act play "Toccata" at the Jean Cocteau Theatre in New York). He has performed in nightclubs and cabarets, at elementary schools, high schools, colleges and universities throughout the Northeast, and if you're lucky you might be able to catch his curbside performance near the entrance to Central Park on a sunny summer day. He teaches classes in mime, clowning and circus skills at his own studio when in New York.

You're never too young or too old—too fat or too thin—too small or too tall—to take part in this vital, lively form of theatre!

And you don't need a theatre company (you don't even need a theatre)—or a play (you "write" one yourself)—or a part (you create your own)! You can perform Mime any time and any place that you choose, and even make money doing it!

With the step-by-step directions in this very clear, creative book, you'll learn valuable technical exercises that will develop your Mime skills; you'll learn how to put together your own material; and you'll learn a great deal about acting, too, even if you've never been on a stage before!